Help Your Son or Daughter
Study for Success

Help Your Son or Daughter Study for Success

JOYCE P. GALL, PH.D.

in collaboration with

MEREDITH D. GALL, PH.D.

M. DAMIEN PUBLISHERS

Eugene, Oregon

Copyright © 1985 by M. Damien Publishers

All rights reserved. No part of this publication may be reproduced, stored in a retrieval system, or transmitted in any form or by any means, electronic, mechanical, photocopying, recording, or otherwise, without the prior permission of the publisher.

Cover Design: Gwen Thomsen
Illustrations: Judy Fairbairn
Composition: Editing & Design Services, Inc., Eugene, Oregon
Production Consultants: Bookmakers, Eugene, Oregon

Manufactured in the United States of America

Address correspondence to:
M. DAMIEN Publishers, 4810 Mahalo Drive, Eugene, Oregon 97405

Library of Congress Cataloging in Publication Data

Gall, Joyce P.
Help your son or daughter study for success.
1. Study, Method of—Handbooks, manuals, etc.
2. Home and School—Handbooks, manuals, etc.
I. Gall, Meredith D., 1942-   II. Title.

LB1049.G345   1985   649'.68   85-1462

First Printing—May 1985
Second Printing—June 1987
Third Printing—August 1987
Fourth Printing— April 1988

ISBN 0-930539-02-8

Dedicated to my parents,

George and Mabel Pershing

Parents of successful students take time to help their children learn.

Preface

Help Your Son or Daughter Study for Success was written for concerned parents who want to help their sons and daughters do their best in school and college. Because it is a guide that suggests specific helping strategies for parents, I refer to it as the *"Parent Guide"* for short.

The *Parent Guide* refers at various points to another book I co-authored, *Study for Success,* which is addressed to students. While doing research for *Study for Success,* I sought the views of many parents as to the secrets of their sons' and daughters' academic success. I discovered that effective parents help their children achieve academic success by various strategies: *coaching, equipping, encouraging, modeling, monitoring,* and *stimulating.*

The *Parent Guide,* written as a companion to *Study for Success,* explains these strategies in depth. It presents 17 recommendations that you can put into use to help your son or daughter learn and apply the *Study for Success* skills. For example, Skill 7 in *Study for Success* is "Do something pleasurable after a study session, not before." In the *Parent Guide,* Recommendation 5 is to reward your student for achieving a study goal *after* it has been met. Thus it reinforces the corresponding student skill.

If you take a minute to review the Table of Contents, you will see the 17 parent recommendations listed. They can be used effectively whether or not your son or daughter is using *Study for Success*. However, I recommend that you obtain a copy of the student book for them if possible. Both *Study for Success* and the *Parent Guide* may be ordered by writing to M DAMIEN Publishers, 4810 Mahalo Drive, Eugene, Oregon 97405. For your assistance, the 80 study skills in *Study for Success* are listed at the end of the *Parent Guide*.

In the past, some of your offers to help with study assignments may have met resistance, or produced tension on both sides. The *Parent Guide* is designed to help you detour around such danger zones and find areas where you can cooperate. If one approach seems inappropriate for your daughter or son, the *Parent Guide* provides other effective approaches to use instead.

The *Parent Guide* suggests that you assist your son or daughter in practicing a few study skills at a time. When your student's study effectiveness improves, he or she will be ready to tackle other study skills.

Soon your daughter or son should display greater confidence and a more positive attitude toward study. Before long you may notice improvements in his or her grades on assignments and tests. And your student will not seem so overwhelmed by school requirements. He or she will be able to study smarter, not harder.

The *Parent Guide* is written from the first author's perspective as an educator, a parent, and a successful student. It has also benefited greatly from the contributions of the second author, Meredith Gall, who helped me organize and flesh out the recommendations. He also wrote the companion book *Study for Success*.

I would like to acknowledge the parents who participated in my research, and the readers of this *Parent Guide,* for helping the students in their families become the best that they can be.

Joyce P. Gall, Ph.D.
January 1985

Contents

Introduction *1*

Recommendations

Provide the Resources Needed for Effective Study

Recommendation 1. Provide nutritious food at meals and for snacks. *5*
Recommendation 2. Provide space and organizers for home study. *6*
Recommendation 3. Schedule time for home study. *7*
Recommendation 4. Provide the study materials and equipment your student needs. *7*

Encourage and Reward School Achievement

Recommendation 5. Reward your student for achieving study goals. *10*
Recommendation 6. Encourage your student to take subjects in school that prepare them for advanced education. *11*

Keep Track of Your Son or Daughter's Progress

Recommendation 7. Help your student establish a study plan and time priorities. *12*
Recommendation 8. Get information from school about your student's progress. *13*
Recommendation 9. Monitor your student's test scores and grades on papers and courses. *14*

Provide Special Learning Experiences

Recommendation 10. Provide experiences that give your student extra exposure to topics covered in school. *15*

Recommendation 11. Encourage your student to seek help if needed. *16*

Set a Positive Example for your Son or Daughter

Recommendation 12. If you have a good system you use to stay organized and get things done, explain it to your student. *18*

Recommendation 13. Show your student how you become well informed about subjects related to your work and personal interests. *19*

Recommendation 14. Share with your student the strategies you use to control tension. *20*

Coach Your Son or Daughter When Necessary

Recommendation 15. Use a variety of techniques to coach your student. *21*

Recommendation 16. Guide your student in mastering new subject matter. *22*

Recommendation 17. Work all the way through several key study skills with your student. *24*

List of 80 Study Skills in *Study for Success* *27*

Concluding Note *43*

Introduction

1. *What is the* **Parent Guide** *for?*

The *Parent Guide* for *Study for Success* suggests specific ways in which you can help your son or daughter learn to use effective study skills. The Guide describes 17 techniques that you can put into practice right away. You are probably using some of these techniques already. Others may be new to you.

Each of the recommendations is effective for a specific purpose. Some of them will be especially appropriate for your son or daughter. Therefore, as you read the Guide, keep your student's special needs and characteristics in mind. Try out first the techniques that will help your student the most.

2. *How does the* **Parent Guide** *relate to* **Study for Success?**

Study for Success was written to help students improve their study skills. The *Parent Guide* is written for parents and other adults, and is much shorter. *Study for Success* includes 80 study skills, while the *Parent Guide* presents 17 recommendations for helping the student learn those skills. The 80 study skills are listed in this Guide to give you a clear picture of what your student will be working on in *Study for Success.*

3. *Is the* **Parent Guide** *only useful for a student's parents?*

This guide is useful for any adult who is committed to helping a student succeed in school. Either a father or mother can use it. A grandparent, older sibling, or close family friend can also use the Guide.

4. *Is my son or daughter the right age for me to make use of the recommendations in this Guide?*

Study for Success was written with three groups in mind —students in junior high school or middle school, high school students, and college students. However, even elementary school students can benefit by learning study skills. With a younger student, you may need to play a more active helping role, so the *Parent Guide* should be very useful. If you work actively on your child's study skills when he or she is young, your assistance may be less necessary later on.

It is never too early for a student to learn study skills — and never too late. If your student is already in graduate school, or has enrolled in a program of adult education, he will still find many good ideas in *Study for Success*. Similarly, this *Parent Guide* can be used as long as your son or daughter is willing to accept your help and expression of interest. Learning is a lifelong process, and so is parenting.

5. *If my own education is limited, can I still use these recommendations?*

My own parents did not complete high school, but they had enthusiasm for education and a desire for all their children to go to college. Their desire was realized: my two sisters and I graduated from college, and two of us also earned advanced degrees (the M.A. and Ph.D.). Most of the recommendations in this Guide do not depend at all on your own level of education or academic ability. As long as you are motivated to have your son or daughter be a successful student, you can make use of the recommendations.

6. What if I am already following some of the **Parent Guide's** recommendations?

I know that parents use many of the techniques I recommend. In fact, the *Parent Guide* recommendations are based on my research with parents, finding out from them what they did that was most helpful to their children's scholastic success. I found that many parents were deeply interested in supporting their students' success in school. However, none of them were following all 17 of these recommendations. If you are already using some of these techniques, congratulate yourself for the contribution you are making to your son or daughter's success. Then turn to the recommendations you are not yet following, and try some of them.

7. What do I do if I try a recommendation and it does not work?

First ask yourself, why didn't it work? If your student resists your help and suggestions, then you need to talk with him or her about that problem. On the other hand, perhaps your student will accept your help but his or her skills will not seem to improve. In this case, try a different recommendation in the Guide — there are plenty! Or wait a while, and try the recommendation again at a later time. For learning to happen, there must be readiness. Be patient; do not give up; and vary your approach.

8. How can I possibly follow all of these recommendations?

As I said earlier, these are ideas I learned from talking to many parents and students. No parent follows all of the recommendations. Most parents are very busy people. Pick the recommendations that suit your time availability and skills, and your student's needs at this time. Later on, try some others.

9. What guarantees do I have that this will work?

While you can help, your student's success depends upon him or her making the necessary effort. Parents can make a big difference, however. From reading the research on education, being a parent myself, and doing my own research for this *Parent Guide,* I have become convinced that students achieve much more when their parents actively support their efforts.

10. I have several children; why do you refer to "your student"?

To help your children learn study skills, you will probably need to work with them individually, at least some of the time. Not only are their ages probably different, but their learning needs differ too. If you have several children, I encourage you to use the *Parent Guide* with each of them, and to have each of them use *Study for Success.*

Recommendations

Provide the Resources Needed for Effective Study

Recommendation 1. Provide nutritious food at meals and for snacks.

A recent newspaper article singled out "serving breakfast" as one of the eight most important things parents can do to promote their children's school success. It has been found that students who come to school without a good breakfast are at a major disadvantage, and perform less well academically than their better-fed classmates. One school administrator said, "I think it's important that kids start the day with a good breakfast. I think that's the beginning of a good day."

As your son or daughter grows older, you will have less control over their nutrition. Not only will they be eating away from home more often, but they will be more exposed to the different eating habits and attitudes of their friends. However, you can still ensure that they get good nutrition at home. It is also wise to discuss nutrition with your children, and have them read articles or books on the subject.

If students buy their lunch at school, check out the lunch program, talk to your student about the menu, and let them know that it is important to you that they eat good food, whether at home or away from home. For students who take bag lunches, and for after-school snacks, you need to have nutritious but easy-to-prepare foods on hand.

If your son or daughter studies after dinner, you should think about the effects of the meal on your son or daughter's study effectiveness. Skill 9 in *Study for Success* recommends "Schedule study sessions when you feel energy peaks." As you know, digestion takes blood away from the brain and uses it to break down the food that has been consumed. Therefore, your son or daughter should eat far enough in advance of study to ensure that digestion does not affect the study process. Large meals, or hard-to-digest foods, are especially to be avoided before an intensive study session.

Recommendation 2. Provide space and organizers for home study.

Two skills in *Study for Success* are relevant to this recommendation: "Keep your study materials accessible and organized" (no. 11); and "Put loose papers in files, and create an index to them" (no. 12).

I think that every child — indeed, every family member — should have his or her own study or work space in the home. While it is possible to study anywhere, having a fixed spot helps a person build a stronger "mental set" for studying. It also makes the task of keeping study materials organized and accessible much easier. The student can arrange needed materials in the study space, instead of having to dig them up and carry them around each time he wants to study.

You can help your son or daughter tremendously by buying them the right equipment for their study space. The right desk and desk lamp will pay off continually by giving your student a comfortable, effective place to do school work and study. Arrange screens or furniture as visual and sound buffers.

Study for Success recommends that your son or daughter use a metal or cardboard file cabinet and file folders to store various study projects (Skill 12). This would be an excellent gift from you at the end of the school year, at Christmas, or as a reward for some special achievement.

As housing costs have risen, many products have become available to help people organize and make better use of limited space. The smaller the study space, the more important it is that your son or daughter keep it neat and well organized. You can purchase a variety of desk and shelf organizers, suited to an individual student's needs and style, at office or stationery stores. Students are not likely to buy such organizers themselves, so you can help them greatly by purchasing a few of these items for them.

If family members must share study space, help them set up a schedule so that each one has enough time to do what they need to do — typing, writing, reading, etc. You can also help by putting the typewriter or other frequently-used items on a stand so they can be moved out of the way easily. Be sure to provide separate storage space for each family member, no matter how crowded you are. If there are four children and only one bookcase, make sure it is a bookcase with at least four shelves and label each shelf with a different child's name.

Recommendation 3. Schedule time for home study.

One mother I talked to singled this out as her biggest contribution to her children's academic success: "I tried to set a consistent family schedule."

Remember that parents set the pace for family routines. If you keep a fairly consistent routine that includes study time, you will help your student build the habit of study at home.

I recommend that you establish a pattern at home for a regular period of "quiet time" devoted to reading and study (including homework). During the common study time you might have a rule that the TV and phonograph are turned down, or off, and that phone calls are kept to a minimum.

Make sure that all family members and visitors know when study time begins and ends. If your son needs to prepare a book report tonight, ask your daughter to practice her trombone later in the evening, when he is rewarding his progress on the book report with an hour of TV viewing.

Recommendation 4. Provide the study materials and equipment your student needs.

Studying is like carpentry: having the right tools helps you do a better job. The study materials students need to do their job fall into five categories:

1. *Textbooks.* Public schools provide required textbooks for students' use. If your student attends a private school or is in

college, he will probably be expected to purchase the textbooks recommended for his courses.

2. *Essential supplies.* Many items are used regularly in almost every subject. They are inexpensive, but need to be purchased whenever the supply runs out. They include:

Binder paper	Paper clips
Binders and dividers	Pens, pencils
Erasers	Rubber bands
Glue	Staples
Notecards	Tape
Opaque (for typing)	

Besides these standard supplies, your student may need other supplies for certain courses or activities, for example drafting pens, sheet music, or drawing pads.

3. *Standard study equipment.* These items only need to be purchased once. Since they are essential to effective home study, most were described in the section, "Provide space and organizers for home study" (Recommendation 2). They include:

Bookcase	File
Desk or table	Lamp
Desk and shelf organizers	Scissors, ruler, stapler, calculator, tape dispenser

4. *Supplementary materials.* Many books are available to help students gain further understanding of topics studied in school. Workbooks or supplements are published to accompany some textbooks. Books by different authors give students added perspective on the topics covered in textbooks, as noted in Skill 31 in *Study for Success*. Reference books give an overview of many topics, or detailed treatment of certain topics. Among the most useful reference books for students are:

Almanac	Study skills manual
Atlas	Style manual for writing
Dictionary	Thesaurus
Encyclopedia	

5. *Other study equipment.* Although these items are moderately to very expensive, they can greatly aid the study process. For example, a tape recorder is useful for helping a student practice a school speech or presentation. Use of a typewriter contributes greatly to the appearance of school papers and reports. (This use of the typewriter is discussed in *Study for Success,* Skill 60.) Also, a home computer is becoming increasingly desirable, since more and more high schools are specifying computer literacy as a requirement for graduation. Some colleges already include computer use as a routine activity in courses.

Many students try to get by with a minimum of the essential supplies. Their energy and time is wasted by not having the right tool for the job. They are also more likely to hand in sloppy work. Over the years I have learned that these tools are the best possible investment for a student or professional to make. Check to be sure your son or daughter has the necessary textbooks, supplies, and equipment for studying and schoolwork.

Discuss with your student the importance of having the right tools for a job. When your child is young, you will make most of the selection decisions and purchases. When she is more mature, explain these categories and get her involved in selecting the items that are essential, nice to have, and not needed. You may want to give your son or daughter an allowance or small budget for these items, and tell them you expect them to use the money for study-related expenses only. This budget should also cover the expense of making photocopies of reference sources and completed papers (see *Study for Success,* Skills 51 and 60).

As for supplementary materials and other study equipment, analyze the benefits relative to the costs, and decide which ones your student needs. Although these items are generally not essential, they may make the difference between adequate and excellent school performance from your student. You can give these items as rewards for good achievement (see Recommendation 5).

You might consider comparison shopping for some study materials and equipment, or even buy used items. For example, I recently bought a used World Book encyclopedia for my son. I spent several hours and went to a dozen bookstores, but the effort paid off. The set is barely a year old, in beautiful condition, and cost roughly a third of the cost of a new set.

Encourage and Reward School Achievement

Recommendation 5. Reward your student for achieving study goals.

One of the first skills in *Study for Success* is "Do something pleasurable after a study session, not before" (no. 7). You can help your son or daughter learn this habit by yourself providing a reward after your son or daughter has completed a study goal. (The goal might involve a certain *level* of performance, or *improvement* over past performance.)

Young children respond well to simple rewards like going to the store for a treat, watching a favorite TV show, a reward sticker (many designs are available at educational and gift shops), or a comic book. Older students may prefer money for movies and food, records and tapes, etc.

You need to be careful, however, about turning rewards into bribery. In other words, do not have your student's effort require or depend on a reward, especially once they reach high school age. Do not give the message, " *If* you do this, I'll give you something you really want." With older students, it is better to give rewards occasionally, at irregular intervals, in recognition of a job well done. Then the student is not being urged to work just for the sake of a gift; he will learn that you expect good work, but also that you admire and appreciate it.

How can you support your son or daughter when they are *not* doing well? One student I know said that her parents help her by keeping it in perspective when she is doing poorly, and by never "putting her down" about it.

Use tangible rewards sparingly, but be lavish in praise and acknowledgement of your student's accomplishments. These gestures are rewarding because they make your student feel good about himself and about his work. Don't be afraid to say "You did a good job, I'm proud of you." You will know you are overdoing praise if your son or daughter stops reacting positively to your comments, but that is unlikely if you only give honest praise for really good work.

Besides plain "fun" things, sometimes give your student a special learning experience or study tool as a reward. Not only is this recognition for the goals they achieved; such rewards will also help them achieve other study goals. See Recommendations 4 and 10 for examples of such rewards.

Recommendation 6. Encourage your student to take subjects in school that prepare them for advanced education.

Perhaps your son or daughter is not sure they want to go on to college or graduate school at this point. However, they may make this decision at some time. Therefore, you need to encourage your son or daughter well in advance to take the courses in school that will prepare them for further study.

One mother I talked to said she didn't "push" college, but she encouraged her children to take college preparatory courses in school "just so you don't close any doors on yourself." I also suggest that you encourage your son or daughter to talk to people who have attended different institutions of higher learning. They will be able to provide information about such matters as admission requirements and availability and difficulty of different programs. This information should help your student discover the opportunities that advanced education provides, and may help motivate him or her to aim for college.

The college preparatory program in high school includes advanced mathematics, advanced language arts, science, and foreign languages. If your student takes this program, remember two things. First, these are usually the most difficult courses offered, so your student will need to work harder to get good grades than if she took easier subjects. Second, she may need to work overtime in order to fit in other courses she sees as desirable — like music, athletics, and typing.

Assume that your student does decide to take the more difficult college prep program in school. Your assistance will be even more necessary, then, to help him or her use the skills described in *Study for Success*. You can also remind your student that the opportunity to continue one's education in a good institution of higher learning is itself a great reward for good performance in high school.

Keep Track of Your Son or Daughter's Progress

Recommendation 7. Help your student establish a study plan and time priorities.

We live busy lives. As your student progresses through school, ever more activities will compete for his or her time. Help your student plan and set priorities! A serious student needs to plan regularly for two reasons — so that he will not overlook any important tasks, and so that he will not get overwhelmed by too much to do.

To set priorities, have your student first ask questions like these: How many courses do I need to work on this term? What other school activities am I involved in? What outside activities are a regular part of my schedule this term (chores at home, after-school job, church choir, soccer team, etc.)? What other things do I want to do? Suggest that your son or daughter write down all the activities, and add to the list as new ones arise.

Second, ask him or her to compare the activities in terms of importance. Then have him select the most important ones to do, or do first.

Setting priorities often requires a student to do some thinking about life goals. Help your son or daughter clarify their goals. Suggest that they think about how each possible activity contributes to their goals. Also ask them to look at each activity's cost in time, money, or effort. Sometimes a student wants to do something very worthwhile, like star in the school play, but is not aware of the great amount of time this will take. Help your student make realistic time estimates when considering new activities.

Read the description of Skill 13 in *Study for Success* to help your student plan his study schedule. Help him devise a system (for example, note cards) to list his schedule of things to do each day; things coming up in the future (perhaps noted in an appointment book); and goals he wants to work towards now, soon, or over the long term.

Become aware of your son or daughter's study habits in these areas: taking lecture notes and participating in class activities while in class; reading textbooks; writing school papers; and preparing for tests. These four activities are the subject of separate chapters in *Study for Success*.

Become familiar with the skills described in each chapter, so that you can get a sense of the skills on which you should check your student's progress. These should be: 1) ones he has selected to work on, 2) ones which have some specific process or outcome that you can observe, and 3) ones on which he is willing to have your assistance. The following are some examples:

Chapter 3. Active Listening and Participation in Class. Ask your son or daughter to tell you about the strategies they are using to absorb information from lectures and speeches.

Chapter 4. Reading Textbooks Effectively. Read a chapter of your student's textbook that has been assigned. Ask him what questions he has generated about the chapter or what the chapter is about.

Chapter 5. Writing School Papers. Ask your daughter what papers she has due, and when. Check to see whether she has set aside enough time to write each one.

Chapter 6. Taking Tests. Find out your student's test schedule for each term. Check to see whether he has built enough time to study for each test into his study plan.

Recommendation 8. Get information from school about your student's progress.

Ideally your son or daughter discusses school matters with you and brings teacher communications home. I also recommend that you take the time to go and talk to school personnel. Each person has a slightly different perspective. Putting all these perspectives together will give you a better picture of your student's progress.

Ask your student what teachers he is taking classes from each term, since his schedule will probably vary from one term to the next. Talk to as many teachers as possible, but certainly those teaching subjects in which you have concerns about your student's progress. Talk to the counselors and any other staff with whom your student has contact.

Use a two-way dialogue, so that you are also giving the school information to help them do a better job teaching your son or daughter. Be sure to tell the school staff about: 1) your student's unique needs, 2) your interest and concern as a parent, 3) your goals for your student, and 4) your willingness to work with the school to foster your student's learning. If you have time to help at school, I recommend it. It will give you a more complete picture of how your student is doing. It will also clarify what you should do, or recommend that the school do, to further aid your student.

I talked to two mothers, both of whom wanted to help their high school students prepare for college. Both had concluded that the school counselor was not giving their children all the information necessary to select appropriate courses and to research colleges and universities. One mother's solution was to send for catalogs from several nearby institutions. She then gave the catalogs to her son to review. The other mother offered to help the school counselor put up a bulletin board with scholarship information. In the process, this second mother not only provided her son, and his classmates, more information. She also made the counselor more aware of her son as an individual, and of her interest in his progress.

Recommendation 9. Monitor your student's test scores and grades on papers and courses.

To help your student do her best in school, find out all you can about how she is doing now. A report card, or other report of progress, is usually sent home with each student one or more times during each school term. Make sure you know when it is sent, and tell your student you wish to see it.

Final course grades give you a general idea of your student's progress. However, they come too late for you to do anything in case your student needs help. You also need to monitor interim grades and scores.

Important decisions will be made about your student based upon his scores and grades. Should he be advanced, or held back? Would he benefit from a special program? Is he eligible for a scholarship? Find out how your student is doing on tests, papers, and other assignments. Then you will understand the basis for decisions about his school program. More important, you can intervene before a decision is made.

Ask your child when he has papers due, tests, and other assignments in each course. Follow up to see whether your student is preparing for the test or assignment, and has completed it. Then check on the results. Ask to see the work. Note not only the overall grade or score, but also the kinds of items missed or errors made.

If your student has met or passed your expectations, give him praise and encouragement, along with feedback about what you see as the strengths of his work. If, on the other hand, there are problems, provide feedback, and encourage him to increase his efforts.

Provide Special Learning Experiences

Recommendation 10. Provide experiences that give your student extra exposure to topics covered in school.

Suppose your daughter tells you she has to write a paper for her Social Studies class, and she is is interested in Japan. Her textbook devotes ten pages to Japan, past and present. She knows she will need to explore other sources of information.

What do you do? In line with Recommendation 4, you can provide her with other written sources. She might read the section on Japan in your home encyclopedia, or borrow a book of Japanese poetry you own. Another idea is to buy her a copy of *Shogun,* or other book on Japan. Thus she will read several sources on the same topic, as recommended in the discussion of Skill 31 of *Study for Success.*

You can also help your daughter learn about Japan by providing her with direct experience of many kinds. Perhaps you live in an urban area where a large number of Japanese people live. If so, take your daughter to visit Japanese shops and restaurants. If you have Japanese friends, arrange for your daughter to meet them.

Almost any everyday experience you have with your student in the ordinary course of events can be tied into what he is learning in school. A news story about relations between the U.S. and Russia could lead to a discussion about the geography and history of the U.S.S.R. Perhaps you are taking your son along on a grocery shopping trip. Discuss the food you select in relation to biology (nutritional requirements of humans) or economics (why prices of certain foods rise or fall), or even geography (food preferences in different cultures or climates).

It is not necessary that every shared experience be related back to school. But used in moderation, this recommendation should aid your student's learning, and help him see its relevance to real life.

Recommendation 11. Encourage your student to seek help if needed.

As early as possible, teach your son or daughter that help is available for difficult learning situations. In at least four situations, a student is wise to get help from others:
1. He has challenging assignments in a course in which he is doing well.
2. He is having trouble handling a particular subject.
3. He is ready for advanced work in a subject.
4. He wants to learn some skills and knowledge not covered in his regular courses.

This list makes clear that asking for help, or taking an extra class, is not necessarily a sign of trouble. All it means is that your

Parent Guide

student needs something beyond just going to class and doing assignments by herself. Often, the best students seek help soonest and most often. Make sure your son or daughter realizes this.

The following are common sources of help available to students:

1. You or a relative. Say your daughter wants to learn computer skills. If you have any background in using computers, share your knowledge with her. Or if Uncle Joe just bought a computer, ask him to invite her over to work on it with him. A student can also learn a great deal from siblings, especially an older sister or brother who has already dealt with the subject.

2. Teachers. If your son is having a hard time in his algebra class, or wants to try some advanced problem sets, suggest he talk to his algebra teacher. Teachers may not be able to provide individual guidance to every student, but they will usually help students who ask for help.

3. Librarians. Whenever your student is writing a paper, ask whether she has talked to a librarian. Besides the school librarian, many cities have libraries. Specialized libraries can be found on any college or university campus, and the librarians there will also aid younger students. Skill 50 in *Study for Success* involves consulting the librarian for help when doing research for a school paper.

4. Classmates. Skill 8 in *Study for Success* recommends seeing a classmate when one has difficulty, rather than procrastinating. Skill 38 suggests asking a classmate who is doing better than oneself for tutorial help if one is having trouble with a subject. Both Skill 8 and Skill 68 discuss the benefits of forming a study group with other classmates to learn a difficult subject, and when preparing for a test.

5. Tutors. Tutors have special expertise in a given subject and are also skilled in helping others learn the subject on a one-to-one basis. *Study for Success* discusses use of a tutor in Skills 8 and 38. Tutors are very helpful for required subjects in which a student is having difficulty.

6. Others. For each topic studied in school, there are usually experts who have studied the topic, or people who have direct experience with it. For example, if your son is writing a paper on the hospice movement, he might talk to medical experts and managers of hospice programs. He might also talk to members of families whose loved ones have been cared for in a hospice.

7. Classes. Classes on many special subjects are available in numerous locations. These include other schools in your area, community colleges, continuing education or noncredit courses at nearby universities, city- or county-run community centers, private companies, and churches. For example, your student might take a typing class at school, even though he is in the college prep program. Typing skills are useful for preparing school papers (see Skill 60 in *Study for Success*); for using a computer; and as a possible means of income to earn money for further schooling. Skill 23 in *Study for Success* recommends taking a communications course to improve one's speaking skills.

Another example comes from a father I know. When his daughter entered high school, she did not feel equipped for the heavy study and assignment demands she now faced. The father enrolled her in a class on study skills at our local community college.

Set a Positive Example for Your Son or Daughter

Recommendation 12. If you have a good system you use to stay organized and get things done, explain it to your student.

Effective study and academic excellence depend on being well organized. If you are well organized in some areas of life, share your strategies with your son or daughter.

You have probably spent years developing your system for getting things done. It may be a simple system, but more likely it has many aspects. For example, your system may relate to keeping track of your time commitments, producing results in your work, keeping your home in order, or pursuing your personal interests.

Select one of these areas, and show your student the strategy you use to handle it. Do you use "To Do" lists, or an appointment book? Do you keep files? Where do you store materials you use in your work or hobbies, and why? How do you plan a large project? Explain these matters at a point when your student is striving to become more organized in his study and school work. They will surely suggest strategies he can adapt.

Another idea is to examine the skills for "Getting Started" in *Study for Success*. These skills are especially relevent to staying organized and getting the job done. Pick a few of the skills that are similar to your own successful strategies. Then show your son or daughter the connection between your situation and their situation in school. For example, "Spend some time on study each day so work does not pile up" (Skill 1) might translate in your own situation as "Do some work on your current projects every day."

Motivation and commitment are usually at the heart of any good system for getting things done. Share your enthusiasm for what you do and the goals you are aiming toward. Explain the part that patience and persistence play in producing the results you want. Perhaps you are someone who must struggle to stay organized, or perhaps this comes easily for you. Either way, help your student understand the strategies you use to get organized and keep at a task until it is done.

Recommendation 13. Show your student how you become well informed about subjects related to your work and personal interests.

If you expect academic excellence from your child, become a model of lifelong learning yourself. This does not mean that you must have a string of academic degrees. Nor do you need to pursue formal education. However, you must show in your own life that you value learning and inquiry.

In every area of life, we can choose to be observers, casual players, or serious students. Research shows that children who grow up in a home filled with books and magazines tend to be better readers, and generally more intelligent, than children whose homes are devoid of reading matter. I doubt that this finding is simply a case that the children read the books and magazines and thus gain knowledge. More likely, the parents read the books and magazines, express informed opinions, and stimulate their children to do the same.

To foster your students' learning, be an active learner yourself. Discuss your interests and opinions with your student regularly, and express interest in his or her views. Whether or not you become actively involved as a coach of your student's learning, your own level of active learning will probably "rub off" on him or her. Also, reading and learning widely will make you much better able to help your student when he or she needs your help.

My parents set a wonderful example of lifelong learning for me. As a child I remember their discussions with visitors, in which the children could join. They were intensely interested in history and current events. Although they had little education, they read a great deal, both novels and non-fiction. Their expression of views conveyed an awareness that there was always more to learn about a subject, and a respect for that learning.

Recommendation 14. Share with your student the strategies you use to control tension.

One of the nicest things about finishing graduate school was knowing that I would no longer have to take tests. But test taking served some useful purposes. First, it enabled others to objectively judge my ability. Second, it helped me realize that no matter how bad I felt, I could complete the test, and move on.

In your current life, you probably do not face school-type tests unless you are enrolled in an education program. However, you probably do face challenges that give rise to tension in most people — getting a performance review at work, giving a talk to your club, completing a marathon.

Let your son or daughter know that you, too, feel tension when you are anticipating a stressful event. This has two benefits. First, it helps your student realize that it is normal to get anxious over a test and that he needs to confront and handle his anxiety. Tests may end when he finishes school, but other stressful challenges will probably continue to come up.

There is also a second benefit of telling your student about your own tension-reducing experiences. The strategies you have discovered to reduce your tension may also work to reduce your son or daughter's test anxiety. *Study for Success* describes several methods (see Skill 62) for controlling test anxiety — exercise, controlled breathing, deep muscle relaxation, positive thinking, meditation, and overpreparation. Tell your student about specific incidents when you used one of these or some other method successfully.

Coach Your Son or Daughter When Necessary

Recommendation 15. Use a variety of techniques to coach your student.

If you decide to coach your son or daughter, you must take on an active teaching role. Use several teaching techniques, rather than relying on one technique exclusively.

I recommend using a variety of coaching techniques for three reasons. First of all, you will not discover the approach that is most helpful to your student if you stick with just one approach. Even if it works, something else might be better. Second, having different kinds of experiences with the same subject matter aids learning (see Skill 31 in *Study for Success*). Each technique you use exposes the problem to a slightly different light.

Finally, you need to avoid getting into a rut when you coach your daughter or son. Vary your approach, to make it more interesting for your student, and for you too.

Here is an example of varying your technique. Say that your student is taking a difficult math course. He complains that he listens carefully to the teacher's explanation of concepts in class, and grasps it, but later he forgets what was discussed. You suggest that he focus on improving his note-taking skills.

After his next math class, you ask if he took notes and get a "Yes!" answer. So you ask him questions about the teacher's lecture. Your questions focus on points in the lecture that he should listen for and record in his notes. Thus you provide a framework for your student's active listening. For example: "What topic was being explained?" "Did the teacher expect you to remember how a mathematical formula was derived?" "Were you expected to know how to apply the formula to solve mathematical problems?" "Was an assignment given? What were you asked to do, and by when?"

By listening to your son's responses, you should get a sense of how well he took notes. After a couple of weeks, try another technique. Ask your son to give you his lecture notes from the last two or three math classes. Review them and comment on them in writing, just as if the notes were a paper you were critiquing.

After using these and other techniques, you should have had some success in improving your son's note taking, and hopefully his math performance. Even if you are not yet satisfied with his skill level, you will have a much clearer picture of his performance. Based on this knowledge, you can more confidently recommend some other approach to improving his note-taking skill, for example, getting help from a classmate, or reading and studying the topic of each lecture more thoroughly beforehand.

Recommendation 16. Guide your student in mastering new subject matter.

Helping students learn subject matter is one of the ways that most parents aid their students' learning. In your own education, you learned much of the material your student will be expected to learn. It is quite natural to share your knowledge and skills as he becomes ready to learn it.

At its simplest, this suggestion involves answering your daughter or son's factual questions, like "At what temperature does water boil?" or "What are the three branches of U.S. government?" When your student needs a fact, save her the trouble of looking it up if you know the answer.

For the many questions that do not have factual answers, we suggest that you share your opinions, as well as specific facts you know that bear on them. Perhaps your son asks, "How did the Vietnam war start?" Express your own views, but point out that not everyone agrees on the causes of that war. Describe some of the differing views people have on this issue, and mention the key events you remember that influenced you in forming your own views.

One of the students I interviewed said his parents help him academically by asking him questions when he is studying for a test. This technique can be used regularly as a way to help your student master new subject matter.

Your student will be expected to learn many concepts and strategies for dealing with each academic subject. If it is a subject in which you yourself are skillful, offer to coach him. For example, my husband is coaching our son in basic mathematical concepts. Jonathan is already doing work beyond his grade level, but seems ready for more. Meredith recently taught him the concept of regrouping, to increase his understanding of borrowing in subtraction.

If your student is not keeping up with academic expectations, coach her to help her catch up. Perhaps, instead, she meets or exceeds the school's standards. In that case, teach her advanced concepts and strategies to help her reach her maximum potential.

A note of caution is in order. In coaching, your goal is to help your student learn how to deal with schoolwork on his own, not to do it for him. An old saying goes: "Give me a fish, and I will eat for today; teach me to fish, and I will eat for the rest of my life."

You should not deny your student help in mastering new subject matter. However, you will be doing him an even greater service by coaching him in learning key study skills. Once he learns these skills, he will be able to master new material and do assignments more effectively, with less direction from others.

Recommendation 17. Work all the way through several key study skills with your student.

One of the hardest things about study is that it takes a long time to reach the goal. Help your son or daughter see that they can only improve one step at a time, not all at once. Then work all the way through some of the study skills with your student. This will help them learn the discipline of working patiently toward a seemingly far-off goal.

Study for Success defines 80 specific study skills. If your student attempts to learn them all at once, she may soon become overwhelmed by the job of improving her study habits. Then she is likely to put off working on them. If, however, she picks a few skills—those which she needs most to succeed in her current school work—she will see positive results sooner. This positive experience will help build momentum for acquiring other study skills.

Help your student select a few critical skills to work on by asking:

1. Which study skills are most in need of improvement? Say that your student writes good papers, but her essay exam answers are poorly written. She admits to having high test anxiety before every exam, which interferes with her ability to write in a timed, closed-book exam. Recommend that she first work on the skills related to test taking. The skills on writing school papers can wait. Similarly, before a certain grade level, your student may not be asked to write scholarly or technical papers. In that case, she will not need the skills for doing library research (Skills 50-54) until later in her schooling.

2. Which study skills are most necessary to reach a goal? Your student may have a difficult assignment to do. Ask him to think through the skills most needed to do the assignment, and the best order in which to learn them. For example, before he writes the first draft of a paper (Skill 48), he needs a clear statement of the topic (Skill 45) and a working outline (Skill 49). If your daughter suffers from severe test anxiety, suggest that she first work on Skill 62 (ways to control test anxiety) and hold off on Skills 63-65, which require her to analyze, cooly, the requirements of a particular test.

3. Which study skills are most likely to produce quick results? Your student should first tackle the skills that give them a positive experience fairly quickly, so that they are motivated to continue.

A friend's son used to get very uptight whenever he had to write a paper. When my friend looked into the problem, she discovered that he was trying to compose on one little corner of his desk, leaving the rest cluttered with books, binders, and personal items. Not only did this limit his work space; it also exposed him to many potential distractors. So my friend helped her son organize his materials and get them off the desktop (see Skill 11 in *Study for Success*). Once he had mastered this skill, he was able to tackle the writing task in a better frame of mind.

After your student selects a skill to focus on, help him work all the way through it. First demonstrate the skill yourself, then have him practice it, and give him feedback. Go through this cycle a few times until he is confident that he knows how to use the skill.

Here is an example. If your daughter tends to procrastinate, she may want to pick Skill 4 as a good place to start: "Break a big task into small, manageable tasks." Help her work through that skill in relation to a particular assignment. Perhaps an English paper is due next week. Guide her in breaking the assignment down, perhaps like this:
 1. Decide on a topic.
 2. Ask the school librarian to help me find some reference sources.
 3. Read at least three sources.
 4. Outline the paper.

... and so on. Let her do as much of the breaking down as she can, and then guide her in spotting any critical tasks that she skipped. For example, ask if she thinks it would be a good idea to read the home encyclopedia entry on her topic before going to the library. Also remind her that *Study for Success* recommends making copies of her reference sources after reading each one (Skill 51). If she agrees, have her add reading the encyclopedia entry as a task between steps 1. and 2. above, and making copies as a task between steps 3. and 4.

List of 80 Study Skills *in* Study for Success

GETTING STARTED

Skill 1. Spend some time on study each day so work does not pile up. Avoid getting behind in your studies, because it then becomes difficult to catch up. You can reserve one or two days a week to let your mind rest completely. On all other days, spend some time on each of your courses and current assignments.

Skill 2. When given a study assignment, do some work on it right away. Get actively involved with your study assignments as soon as you receive them. Simply reading over the assignment and jotting down your first ideas or gathering necessary materials helps to get your mind in gear.

Skill 3. Maintain continuity of study, so you do not lose the thread. If a study project is interrupted for more than a few days, you may forget where you are on it. Then you must spend extra time warming up to the task again. You can avoid this problem by spending some time on the study project each day. Label and store your materials so you can easily pick up the project where you left off.

Skill 4. Break a big task into small, manageable tasks. If a study assignment is too long to complete in one session, the temptation is to put it off until later. Consequently, you may have to rush and cut corners to get it in on time. A better approach is to analyze a large assignment into many small tasks. Then make each small task a goal for one study session.

Skill 5. Set minimal goals for each study session. If you set an unrealistically high goal for your study session, you may be tempted to avoid the task. Or you may fail to achieve the goal, which can discourage you from further effort. Instead, set a minimal goal that you can easily achieve. This will make it easy for you to get started.

Skill 6. Set reasonable standards for your initial efforts on an assignment. Anxiety about meeting high standards is a common source of study procrastination. You can avoid this problem by just getting started on the assignment, working informally. Once you have a first version done, your mind should be at ease. You can then revise the first version to improve its quality.

Skill 7. Do something pleasurable after a study session, not before. Since study is hard work, you need to build in immediate rewards for your efforts. If you engage in pleasant activities *before* study, however, your motivation to study may disappear. Instead, use pleasurable experiences as a payoff for achieving your study goals.

Skill 8. If you get stuck on an assignment, see a teacher, classmate, or tutor. If you do not know how to tackle an assignment, ask someone for help (for example, a teacher, another student, or a special tutor). Another good idea is to pool your wits with your classmates by forming a study group.

Skill 9. Schedule study sessions when you feel energy peaks. Analyze your unique patterns of mental energy and fatigue. Schedule study periods when your enegy level is high. Take study breaks or do mentally nontaxing tasks when your energy is low.

Skill 10. Use relaxation techniques and exercise to put yourself in a positive mood for study. Distraction and stress make studying difficult. You can relax by meditating or focusing on your breathing just before you begin a study session. Also, sports or exercise are good for increasing your reserves of mental energy, so that you are then better prepared to study.

Skill 11. Keep your study materials accessible and organized. If your study materials are disorganized, you may tend to avoid studying or waste time trying to find what you need. Make sure you have enough surface space to store each of your active study projects. Allocate time regularly to clean house and re-organize your study materials.

Skill 12. Put loose papers in files, and create an index to them. A metal file cabinet and three-cut letter-size file folders are a good investment for keeping organized. Label your files, and create an index to them for quick, easy reference.

Skill 13. Set aside time each day for planning your studies. Careful planning is necessary to keep track of your priorities and to schedule time for getting them done. Keep a list of your daily schedule and appointments, and carry it with you. Plan not only your daily schedule, but also take time for weekly and long-range planning.

ACTIVE LISTENING AND PARTICIPATION IN CLASS

Getting the Most from Lectures

Skill 14. Take notes when it is important to remember what the teacher is saying. To determine what you should take notes on, analyze the teacher's intentions. When the teacher expects you to remember what is said in class for a test or assignment, take careful notes. Also be sure to take notes when the teacher presents course assignments and procedures. When the teacher does not expect you to remember what is being said, you can just listen attentively.

Skill 15. Read the assignment before coming to class. When teachers lecture in class, they usually assume that you have read your textbook assignment beforehand, and so are already familiar with certain technical terms and ideas. To get the most from the teacher's lectures, therefore, read the assignment before the teacher lectures on it.

Skill 16. Take selective notes on the teacher's lecture. Taking too many notes interferes with your ability to listen to the teacher's presentation. You can avoid this problem by taking selective notes that emphasize the teacher's most important points. In this way you have the time to listen and think about what the teacher is saying.

Skill 17. Make a brief summary at the end of the lecture. To get the "big picture" of what the teacher's lecture was about, spend a few minutes at the end of class writing a brief summary. Identify the main topics and ideas. Keep the summary with your lecture notes for that class, to help you prepare for tests or writing assignments.

Skill 18. Write your lecture notes on binder paper. Keep your studies organized by putting everything for a particular course in one place: lecture notes, teacher handouts, magazine articles, etc. For this purpose, buy a 3-ring binder and 8½" × 11" binder paper for taking lecture notes. When necessary, punch holes in other materials so that they can be integrated with your notes in the binder. Also, use binder dividers so that you can organize the materials needed for all of your courses in one binder.

Skill 19. Ask questions in class. Even if the teacher does not invite students to ask questions, feel free to raise your hand when you want him or her to clarify something. Do not let fear of the teacher, other students' reactions, or speaking up keep you from asking your question. Asking questions requires you to think actively about the course content, so it is a smart thing to do.

Participating in Class Discussions

Skill 20. Read the assignment beforehand so you can contribute to class discussions. If you have already read the assignment being discussed in class, you are more likely to have a pertinent fact or opinion to contribute. You will also be better prepared to respond if the teacher calls on you to answer a question.

Skill 21. Rehearse what you want to say before you say it. When you participate in a discussion, try these steps: Listen attentively, get an idea, rehearse the idea mentally to see if you can state it clearly, and when you are ready to express your idea, signal non-verbally that you wish to speak.

Skill 22. If you do not feel comfortable expressing an opinion, ask a question. Perhaps there are times when you are unsure of your own opinion, but still wish to contribute to a class discussion. When this occurs, ask a pertinent question, directed at the teacher or another student.

Skill 23. Improve your speaking skills by taking a communications course. Many students feel uncomfortable speaking in their classes or other group situations. If you are such a student, you can gain skill and confidence in speaking by taking a communications course offered at your school or college.

READING TEXTBOOKS EFFECTIVELY

A Strategy for Reading Textbooks

Skill 24. Start your study of a textbook chapter by reading the headings and subheadings. Rather than reading a textbook chapter straight through, start by reading all of the main headings and subheadings in the chapter. Doing this will give you a good overview of what the entire chapter is about. Jot down the headings briefly in your notes, using the notes to help you reflect on what the chapter is about.

Skill 25. After reading each section of a chapter, generate questions about its content. As soon as you have read the material under one chapter heading or subheading, write down some questions about it. Ask questions that will require you to remember the important facts and ideas from the material. Write the questions on the left side of a binder page, leaving room for brief answers on the right side.

Skill 26. Write definitions of key terms. When you come to a new term in your reading assignment, write it down. Also write a definition of the term, putting it in your own words so that it makes sense to you personally. When possible, write an example that helps to define the concept for you.

Skill 27. Ask yourself questions about relationships depicted in graphs, tables, and diagrams. Numerical data in textbooks are often presented in graphs or tables. To understand them, it helps to ask yourself two questions. First, what are the things that are shown in the graph or table? Second, what is the relationship between these things? These same questions apply to non-numerical data presented in a diagram.

Skill 28. Write down the questions you have generated. An alternative to taking notes is to keep a written record of the questions that come to mind as you read a textbook. At the top of a binder page, write the section heading from the textbook and the pages it includes. Then write your questions on the left side of the page. On the right side, jot down brief words or phrases that answer the question.

Skill 29. Asterisk your most important questions for intensive review. After generating questions for an entire textbook chapter, go through them again. Put an asterisk next to the most important questions (no more than one fourth of the total). This process helps you to think more deeply about the textbook content.

Skill 30. Use time lines and concept trees to organize your textbook study. A time line lists a sequence of related events in their order of occurrence. Concept trees show the logical relationships between concepts. Make up time lines and concept trees to help you form a "big picture" of details in a textbook chapter or series of chapters.

Skill 31. Investigate several sources on the same topic. To increase your understanding of difficult but essential topics in your textbook, read other sources on the same topic. You can also enrich your understanding by other kinds of experiences, like movies, visits to museums, and interviews with experts.

Skill 32. Read at your normal rate of speed. Active mental processing of what you read is more important than reading speed. If you read at least 300 words a minute with good comprehension, you probably do not need to increase your reading speed. If you read less than 200 words a minute, however, seek professional help to increase your reading speed.

Skill 33. Rely on your own notes and questions, not on other students' work. Some textbooks provide summaries and questions at the end of each chapter. Or perhaps you have access to notes prepared by another student. Even when these aids are available, you should supplement them by generating your own questions and notes. In this way you ensure that you have engaged in active mental processing of the material.

Scholarly and Research Texts

Skill 34. Make notes on the major assertions and conclusions in primary source documents. Textbooks are secondary sources, which review and interpret original documents. The original documents are primary sources. When you read primary sources, make a list of the author's assertions, generalizations, and conclusions. Also take notes on the evidence or arguments used to support them. When appropriate, make comparisons between the primary source document and other sources relating to the same topic.

Studying Literature

Skill 35. Attend to the literary aspects of literature. When studying a piece of literature, take notes on the following literary aspects: author's point of view, recurrent themes, character development, and use of such literary devices as metaphor, symbolism, and irony.

Skill 36. Read critical reviews of literary works to increase your understanding of literature. Essays and books written by literary critics present facts and interpretations that can increase your understanding of literature. For your most important literature assignments, read a few such reviews. If you include ideas from the reviews in your papers, acknowledge the source in your citations.

Science and Mathematics Textbooks

Skill 37. Do not skip any section of a math-based textbook that you do not understand. If you find advanced math and science textbooks to be technical and difficult, plan to spend more time reading such textbooks, not less. When you encounter an equation or concept you do not understand, turn back in your reading rather than go on. Re-study the concepts presented earlier that are needed to understand the section that confused you.

Skill 38. Get tutorial help if you need it. If you get hopelessly confused while studying a math or science textbook, it is time to seek help. Ask a classmate or your teacher for aid. You might even consider hiring an advanced student to give you individual tutoring.

Skill 39. Make sketches to help you solve mathematical problems. Math and science textbooks often present verbal descriptions of a problem to be solved. Try making a sketch to represent visually all the important information in the problem. The sketch can help you derive an equation or set of equations to solve the problem.

WRITING SCHOOL PAPERS

Skill 40. Examine good papers written by other students. A good way to learn how to write well is to watch an expert writer at work. If this is not possible, do the next best thing: observe the product of the writer's efforts. Try to obtain examples of well-written papers from your teachers, classmates, or relatives.

Skill 41. Have a step-by-step plan for writing your paper. Tackle writing assignments one step at a time: identify your topic, make notes of your ideas, do library research if necessary, make an outline, write a first draft, have someone review your first draft, revise the paper, repeat the process of review and revision as many times as you think necessary, and have the final version of the paper typed.

Skill 42. Allow a substantial amount of time for writing a course paper. Good course papers require a substantial amount of time to plan and write. For example, a typical 15-page paper assigned for a college course can take 25 or more hours to plan, research, write, revise, and type. Be sure you allocate enough time to do the job.

Skill 43. Hand in your paper on time. Plan your time so that your paper is sure to be finished by the due date. Many teachers will penalize a late paper by assigning it a lower grade.

Skill 44. Analyze the paper assignment carefully. When you receive a writing assignment, read it carefully to identify the topic, points to cover, format, and length. If this information is not given, ask the teacher for it.

Skill 45. State your paper topic as an intellectual task you will accomplish. Instead of writing about a "thing," define your paper topic as a thought-provoking problem to be solved or task to be accomplished. For example, you can: "Make comparisons between..."; "Evaluate and criticize..."; "Explore the consequences of...." Stating topics this way provides direction to the type of library research and organization your paper will require.

Skill 46. State the purpose of the paper in the first paragraph. To get your paper started, write a statement beginning with the phrase, "The purpose of this paper is to (demonstrate, examine, analyze)...." This statement specifies the intellectual task you plan to accomplish. Next write a few sentences that further describe the task and explain its importance. Use these sentences to start the paragraph and conclude with your "The purpose..." sentence.

Skill 47. Use brainstorming to develop ideas for your paper. Brainstorming enhances your creativity by requiring you to alternately suspend and apply critical judgment. To use brainstorming in writing your paper, first define the topic or task. Second, think of as many ideas as you can. At this stage, suspend judgment and let your ideas flow, "piggy backing" to let one idea build on another. Third, use critical judgment to select the best ideas from all those you generated.

Skill 48. Use a conversational tone when you write the first draft of a school paper. Do not worry about achieving a polished, formal tone when you start writing your paper. Just write the first draft in a natural, informal style, as if you were speaking aloud. Once you have a first draft, you can revise it if necessary to a more formal style.

Skill 49. Write from an outline. To help organize your thoughts, make a simple outline before you begin to write. List all the major points you wish to make and put them in the order that you will present them. Then make a mini-outline of what you wish to say about each major point, and use the mini-outline to help you write that section of the paper.

Skill 50. Consult the librarian for help when doing library research. Talk to a librarian for help in identifying the best library resources for your writing assignments. Librarians know about many sources of information that you would not ordinarily find by just using the library catalog.

Skill 51. Make copies of your reference sources. You do not need to make extensive notes on reference material that you find in the library. It is much easier to make a photocopy of it. Be sure to note the source of the material somewhere on the photocopy so that you can cite it properly in your paper.

Skill 52. Include ideas from library sources in your paper. If you have done library research in writing your paper, include your findings in the paper. Try to blend in the references with your own writing, and place all the footnotes together at the end of the paper. Do not use many direct quotes; when appropriate, paraphrase the quote and cite its source.

Skill 53. Keep track of bibliographic information on references you cite. You should cite in your paper the library sources from which you obtained facts and ideas. Therefore, record the source of each idea or quote that you might want to include in the paper. For an article, write down the author, title, name of the journal or magazine, volume number, date, and page numbers. For a book, record the author, title, publisher, edition number, and copyright date. Note the page numbers of any material that you intend to quote.

Skill 54. Start writing while doing library research. In practice, the steps of writing a paper overlap each other. After doing some library research, outline your paper and start the first draft. Then continue doing library research on an "as needed" basis.

Skill 55. Get distance from your first draft by asking yourself questions about it. After you finish your first draft, read it through. Ask yourself such questions as: "Will this sentence be clear to the reader?" and "Can I state this idea more concisely?" Set aside a block of time to revise your first draft based on your answers to these questions.

Skill 56. Ask another person to review your first draft. You can get "distance" from your first draft by having someone (perhaps a parent or fellow student) read it and give you critical feedback. Be sure to use the feedback in revising your paper.

Skill 57. Work on technical aspects of your paper in the second draft. Try and write at least two drafts of your school papers. In the first draft, focus on what you want to say. In the second draft, revise your paper to remove technical weaknesses such as:

incomplete sentences, spelling errors, overly long paragraphs, poor choice of words, odd sentence construction, vague referents, and wrong choice of tense or tense agreement.

Skill 58. Use headings in your paper. Headings can improve the organization and appearance of your paper. Use center headings to introduce major topics around which the paper is organized. Use side headings to introduce subtopics. Use paragraph headings to introduce topics discussed in a series of paragraphs.

Skill 59. Leave space on your first draft for revisions, or put them on separate sheets of paper. Make minor revisions right on your first draft. Use wide-rule paper, or write your first draft double-space, so that you have room to make changes. Another method is to leave extra-wide margins on the left side of the paper. Lengthy revisions can be written on separate sheets of paper.

Skill 60. Type your paper neatly on good paper. A typed paper makes a positive impression, and it makes the teacher's job easier. In typing your paper: use a high-quality bond paper and typewriter ribbon; type the paper double-space and use appropriate typeface; proofread and correct typing errors; include your name and other identifying information on the front page; and make an extra copy to keep before handing in your paper.

TAKING TESTS

Before the Test

Skill 61. Learn your test schedule early in the term, and plan accordingly. Write the dates of your tests each term in your appointment book, and reserve time for study and review. If the tests for different courses are spaced well, you will have time for rest and last-minute review. If some tests are scheduled back-to-back, you will need to prepare for them carefully in advance. Keep heavy testing periods free for study and review by getting other required work done beforehand.

Skill 62. Control test anxiety by exercise, controlled breathing, deep muscle relaxation, positive thinking, meditation, and overpreparation. Many students experience physical symptoms of anxiety in anticipation of a test. If test anxiety is too high, it will interfere with your test preparation and test performance. Techniques to reduce anxiety include: exercise; taking slow, deep breaths; deep muscle relaxation (systematically tensing and then relaxing each muscle group in your body); positive thinking (consciously holding thoughts about doing well on the test); meditation (clearing your head of all thoughts, or channeling your mental energy into a single focus); and overpreparation (continuing to study until you know the material inside out).

Skill 63. Identify the teacher's testing habits. Learn the types of tests your teacher usually gives: multiple-choice items or essays; focussed on details or on big ideas; and what topics are emphasized. Get hold of previous tests given in your course, if possible. If not, examine tests that your teacher has given in other courses.

Skill 64. Ask yourself questions that you think the teacher is likely to ask. By the time of a test you should have a sense of the teacher's priorities. Use this knowledge to generate questions that you think the teacher is likely to ask on the test. Write out the questions, and brief cues to the answers (a few key words, or the pages in the text where the answers can be found).

Skill 65. Analyze the types of items likely to be on the test. To prepare for a test, ask yourself what kind of learning outcome the teacher expects you to have achieved: recall of information, ability to think, ability to apply skills, or some combination of these. If you think the teacher will test information recall, generate a question for each fact or set of facts that you think you need to memorize. If you expect to be tested for your ability to think and communicate, generate four or five thought-provoking essay questions, each on a different range of course topics. If you will be tested on the ability to apply skills, practice the skills by solving problems similar to those that you think will be on the test.

Skill 66. Balance your textbook review between quizzing yourself, reviewing notes, and scanning the text. Do not try to re-read the entire textbook before a test. Instead, use a combination strategy. Spend the most time making up and answering questions about the text. Also review your notes on the textbook. Finally, scan, rather than read, the textbook.

Skill 67. Memorize rather than use crib sheets. Some students prepare for tests by writing key formulas, events, or other essential information on small pieces of paper called "crib sheets." It is unethical to use these crib sheets during the test. Therefore, if you make crib sheets, memorize the information on them. To improve your memory, use mnemonic devices like making up a sentence using the first letter of each item on the list.

Skill 68. Form a study group to prepare for a test. When studying for important tests, find a classmate or group of students to work with you. Take turns generating and answering questions, and give each other encouragement.

Skill 69. Plan for the supplies you will need for the test. Collect beforehand the supplies you will need during the test. The most commonly needed items are: paper, at least two pencils with erasers or two pens, ruler, calculator, stapler, and something to munch on (if this is allowed). Assemble these supplies the day before the test, so that on test day you do not have to worry about them.

On the Day of the Test

Skill 70. Get to the testing room well in advance. Double-check where and when your test is being given. Also plan to get to the test early, so you will have time to handle any problem that arises at the last minute.

Skill 71. Try to get a comfortable seat near the test administrator. Position yourself in the testing room so that you can avoid such distractions as a noisy corridor and students who mutter, cough, or otherwise disturb others. If the test is being held in a large room, sit near the front so you can hear test directions better, and so you can more readily attract the teacher's attention if you need to ask a question.

Skill 72. Read test directions carefully. Take time before you start answering test questions to read the directions carefully. Pay special attention to instructions about: how to mark your answers, whether you can choose which questions to answer, penalties for guessing, and the point value of different items.

Skill 73. Plan how much time to spend on each section of the test. If the test has a time limit, plan a strategy to ensure that you finish on time. Before you begin, decide how much time to spend on each section of the test. Use these time allocations to pace yourself.

Skill 74. Answer easy test items first to build confidence and momentum. Tackle easy items on the test first. This approach gives you confidence that you can handle the test and a sense of accomplishment. After completing the easy items, go back to the items of medium difficulty. When you finish them, use whatever time is left to answer the most difficult items.

Skill 75. Take mini-breaks during the test. Use short rest breaks to restore your energy as you work through the test. Take 10 or 15 seconds to close your eyes or wipe your face with a moist towelette. If allowed, munch on "energy" food. If you start feeling anxious, try using one of the techniques recommended to reduce test anxiety, such as controlled breathing or positive thinking.

Skill 76. Write an exam essay the same way you would a course paper. Before writing an exam essay, take a few minutes to brainstorm and to make a brief outline. Then start with an introductory paragraph that tells how your answer is organized. Be sure to follow the essay instructions carefully and to keep track of the available time.

Skill 77. In writing exam essays, leave blank spaces for revisions. Write your answers to essay questions in a way that allows you to make revisions on the same sheet of paper. If possible, use wide-ruled paper so that you can write in minor revisions right above the place in the essay where they belong. Also leave several inches of blank space at the top of each page for making more extensive revisions. Draw an arrow from the revision to the place where it is to be inserted in your answer. In this way, everything the teacher needs to read for that essay question is on the same page.

Skill 78. When uncertain of the correct answer to a test item, make a reasonable guess. Note whether there is a penalty for incorrect multiple-choice answers on the test. If not, or if the penalty is small, consider guessing whenever you can eliminate one or more options as incorrect. When you draw a blank on an essay question, skip it rather than write a meaningless response. If, however, you know something about the topic but cannot recall specific facts, give a more general answer.

Skill 79. Double-check that you have answered all test items. In the last few minutes of the test, quickly check to be sure you have not accidentally skipped any items.

Skill 80. Avoid becoming distracted by what other students do during the test. In taking a test, be sure to follow your own game plan. Do not become concerned if you see other students writing longer answers or handing in their tests before you. If you have extra time, re-read the test directions, double-check your answers to multiple-choice items, and think of ways to improve your essay responses.

Concluding Note

The fact that you are reading this *Parent Guide* suggests that you are a parent who has played an active role in your son or daughter's learning. Such a role can be very challenging—and very rewarding too.

As a user of this *Parent Guide*, you can congratulate yourself for having done some or all of the following:

You have *equipped* the students in your family, providing the resources they need for effective study.

You have *encouraged* your daughter or son, giving them rewards and encouragement for school achievement.

You have *monitored* your students' learning, keeping track of their progress.

You have *enriched* your son or daughter's learning, providing special learning experiences for them.

You have *modeled* the value of learning, setting a positive example for your daughter or son.

You have *coached* your son or daughter, giving them specific instructional guidance when appropriate.

The world's knowledge keeps changing and expanding. As a result, your son or daughter will need to become a lifelong learner in order to succeed. The help that you give them with study tasks now will continue to benefit them their whole lives.

6

**Also available from
M DAMIEN Publishers**

STUDY FOR SUCCESS

The Most Essential Study Skills for School and College

Whether you are collegebound, already in college, or in an advanced degree program, effective study skills are your guarantee of success. This important new book will serve as your personal guide to mastering them!

You'll learn:
- How to overcome study procrastination
- How to participate and take notes in class
- How to get the most out of reading material
- How to do writing assignments
- How to take tests

Available in bookstores, or you may order direct from the publisher. For each book ordered, send check or money order (no cash or C.O.D.'s, please) for $7.95 plus $1.25 for postage and handling, to: M DAMIEN Publishers, Dept. A, 4810 Mahalo Drive, Eugene, Oregon 97405. Please allow 4-6 weeks for delivery.

M DAMIEN Publishers
Dept. A, 4810 Mahalo Drive
Eugene, OR 97405

Please send _____ copies of
Study for Success to:

Name _____

Address _____

City _____ State _____ Zip _____

I have enclosed a check or money order for $7.95 plus $1.25 for postage and handling, for each book ordered.